Recognizing Opportunities

on the Path to Success

A Must Read for Anyone Who Wants to Grow in Life and in Business

By:

Barak Levi

Series Name:

Self Fulfillment and Success in Life and in Business

Recognizing Opportunities

on the Path to Success

A Must Read for Anyone Who Wants
to Grow in Life and in Business

E-mail: barakmnlp@gmail.com

Official Website: baraklevi.com

Blog – Discover The Power Within You:

baraklevi.blogspot.co.il

Barak Levi

Author: Barak Levi

Editing and proofreading: Nataly Shohat

Cover design: Lev-Ari Studio

050-2374195

The book was written in a male gender form for convenience purposes,

however, it refers to both men and women.

No Part of this book may be photocopied, recorded, translated, stored in a database, arranged or transmitted in any form or by any means –electronic, optical or mechanical methods existing today.
Commercial use of any type of material included in this book is strictly prohibited without written authorization from the publisher and the author

Table of Contents

Acknowledgements

Thank you to all the people who guided me and helped me during the course of writing my first book **Recognizing Opportunities on the Path to Success**; To the people who taught me and who had a part in the insights I collected along the way and the inspiration I got from them and from my surroundings, as well as coping with my past experiences, accepting and learning from them; To my Dudi Genis for giving me the opportunity to meet Amit Offir – the manager of Rav Mecher Publishing, to develop my writing and to write the book.

I would like to mention in particular two people, which a great part of the insights, ideas and inspiration in the book is thanks to them. Without your tremendous and significant help this book wouldn't be published.

Arie Kegen

You are my mentor and I learn so much from you in every meeting and conversation with you. I thank you for the knowledge and the insights you bestow on me and the great inspiration that comes out of you, from which I also get inspiration. You have opened a wonderful window for me to the world of NLP and personal growth.

Amit Offir

I would like to thank you for the possibility and for the amazing opportunity to write this book. Thanks to you a new book is born with knowledge and inspiration that will teach many people. Thank you for the insights, the ideas and the knowledge you've given me and the guidance for writing this book. This knowledge will serve me when I write many more books in the future.

Clarification

This book was written to help you become a person who recognizes opportunities around him, who thinks correctly, who acquires an abundance consciousness and habits that promote him. All of these will help you move forward towards your dreams and ambitions. This book is meant to enable you to reach new heights, over and over and achieve your goals, objectives and your wildest dreams.

This book contains methods and tools which I myself use. This is not about rumors or research about other successful people – these methods help me recognize the opportunities which come my way and create thoughts and habits for myself which will promote me towards my dream and my vision.

That said, this book is not a promise or a guarantee for your successes.

I cannot promise you anything regarding your abilities to achieve any results using the ideas, methods and the tools I teach and their implementation.

Your success depends solely on your ability **to persist, to implement** the methods and the tools and to find **what works for you and what suites you**, while using good judgment.

The contents of this book is organized in a way that will enable you to examine yourself and the way you conduct yourself in your life and ask yourself if you conduct yourself as a person who has habits that promote or restrict him, as well as to learn how to improve in order to reach better results.

I hope this book will help you change your life and grow, both on a business and personal level and by doing so become a better person.

I thank you for purchasing the book and I will be more than happy to hear your opinion about it. Moreover, I would very much appreciate it if you could find a way to share stories and examples from your personal life with me and if this book helped you, I would be happy if you could recommend others to read it and use its tools.

My contact e-mail address is:

barakmnlp@gmail.com

About the Author

Barak Levi is an NLP practitioner, guides people to success, a lecturer, a personal and business coach an entrepreneur and a mentor for personal and business development with emphasis on the method of NLP.

Barak participated in lectures from masters who are experts in their field, among them are: Arie Kegen, Nik Halik, he also participated in an influence seminar by Julie Silverthorn. Barak develops and creates information products which help many people live a better life and enjoy his unique knowledge. He coaches, personally trains and guides people who want change, a direction in life and an improvement in their abilities.

Barak's unique work methods help many of his customers develop and get ahead in their careers and the areas of interest in which they want to improve and grow, by implementing the methods accurately, persistently, with a desire to win and with personal and business guidance.

Barak is an entrepreneur at heart and develops information and content products in various fields of empowerment, among which are processes of guided imagery in various subjects, writing guides and tools for creating communication with the subconscious, workshops and courses.

Barak can be contact for consultation and personal and business training, for courses, workshops and for lectures in various subjects that are unique to him.

Introduction

The book you are holding in your hand is a result of a few significant events in my life, as well as deepening in the field of NLP. Lately I've started delving into the study of this technique and going through processes with the help of the tools and techniques it teaches.

What is NLP and how is it created?

Two young scientists, a mathematician and a computerist in the name of Richard Bandler and the linguist John Grinder, teamed together in the mid-1960s to answer the question: "how does a change in a person's behavior occur?" and to check whether a specific formula exists for this purpose. Their starting point was observations of a huge number of therapeutic processes which were performed by the biggest therapist in the US at that time: Milton Erickson (1901 – 1980), Virgina Satir (1919-1988) and others.

Richard Bandler was transcribing for Virgina Satir and he noticed that during her treatments in particular a profound change occurs in patients. A person would not come out as he entered, and not only that, with time Richard adopted Virginia's qualities and her speech ability and more.

At that stage Richard teamed with John and they began to further investigate the subject. Their goal was to discover constancy in the ways the therapist influences the patient. They discovered a few laws relating to linguistic, intellectual and neurological components of human behavior, which play an important role in the interaction between the therapist and the patient. They called the model they developed as a result of their findings:

Neuro-Linguistic Programming.

Description:

Neuro – this means the neurological system, the nervous system through which we experience the world, collect and process information received through the five senses.

Linguistic – language (verbal and non-verbal), through which we code and arrange the information and give it meaning. The way and manner in which we express our thoughts and sensations.

Programming – the program or pattern of the behavior. The pattern of thoughts which turn into actions. How is it possible to create a behavioral pattern and program for achieving goals and creating results.

In other words – the patterns, the programs and the strategies which operate in the neurological system and create various actions. How to create communication and understanding with our brain, with the neurological system, communication which can consistently lead to creating results in various fields, achieving goals and a lot more.

NLP is not a new psychological theory, but rather a model which organizes existing phenomena into a significant model which can be easily and efficiently implemented. The efficiency of the NLP model is tested by its success in creating the desired change in behavior and perception.

One of the most effective things about implementing the NLP model in the various aspects of life is the ease of its implementation and the speed of achieving desired results. **"NLP is an attitude and a methodology that leaves behind a trail of techniques".** Richard Bandler.

These processes and techniques that I used caused me to re-examine the most meaningful events in my past and come to terms with them; To examine the present as it is, to check if I'm satisfied with it, to know where I'm heading to and where I want to reach in the future. Thanks to them I found my purpose and what I want to do in life.

I realized that a lot of things bothered me and that wasn't happy about the way I was functioning at the time: the hesitating, the doubting, the fear that I was in. I wanted a change with all my heart and I was ready for it. Along the way and the changes I indeed experienced, I learned a lot and had important insights about the path we walk as individuals and as a group, along with insights about life itself.

Some of the knowledge and the insights are included here, in this book. I hope you'll make the best out of it, as a matter a fact I insist on it.

The book deals with various ways to recognize opportunities in areas that are important to each and every one, from career and business, relationships, fulfillment and dreams to the path to success. Obtaining the opportunities for the promotion of goals, targets, aspirations, dreams and anything else you can think of. The book will teach you to be immersed in abundance consciousness, to know yourself and know what your strongest and deepest desires and aspirations are and to recognize the opportunities and the abundance in the world and in your surroundings for the purpose of their actual fulfillment.

In the book there are tools and new perspectives which I convey from the insights and knowledge I've acquired. I invite you to try and advise you to adopt the tools which you enjoy and which help you. The tools are taken from various methods for personal growth, and most of them, as mentioned, are from the world of NLP. The chapters in the book follow and relate to each other. The tools in the book worked for me and helped me reach considerable personal achievements in a very short period of time.

In the book you will come across stories from my life, which illustrate the power of these tools. These stories have given me important insights about life, were the inspiration for writing this book and sharing them with as many people as possible, so that everyone can achieve more in their lives and so we can create a better world to live in.

How to Make the Most Out of the Book

If you are holding this book in your hands, I assume you want to learn how to recognize the opportunities around you and how to create change in your life – to grow, to get ahead and to achieve more in your career, business, family life, your relationship and the rest of the subjects you face on a daily basis. I appreciate you for it and it doesn't matter how much knowledge and experience you've managed to acquire so far.

It is well known that the ability to learn is a virtue which is associated with successful people. Without the ability to learn humanity would never have survived and most likely would have become extinct already tens of thousands of years ago.

This ability to explore and to thrive has lead humanity to unprecedented records which were broken, over and over, with the help of creative thinking, faith, research, courage and entrepreneurship.

Without these qualities we would have never gotten to the moon, invented the light bulb and created communication with a person who is on the other side of the world.

As social beings, the will to help one another and to help using the information we accumulated is probably ingrained in us, like a father's desire to save his son from the mistake he learned from firsthand.

This power, in my eyes, causes a deeper and stronger process to occur.

In any case, the secret is the desire to learn and know more about the world around you. There are a few ways to read and make use of an informational book such as this. There are people who read the information, summarize, write and implement it in their lives and there are those who read the book like any other book but do not make any practical use out of it.

Either way, you have to be open to learn new information. An effective way to learn and absorb something new is to approach it as a "clean slate", as a person who doesn't know a thing. That way you can retrieve from the book the insights I had from what I learned and from my life in the best possible way.

There are many ways for you to learn and implement the information in the book. The best way to use it, in my opinion, is **to read every subject separately, to mark the parts that interest you with a marker and to write remarks and explanations while reading.** If reading the book evokes a good idea in you, write it in your notebook and go back to it later on.

Tip 1: See this book as a tool as any other tool, which can be written in and marked with no fear, this book is not meant to sit on your book shelf, but to be used as a daily tool.

Tip 2: Arrange in advance for a notebook in which you can write insights, remarks, ideas and any subjects you like, while you read the book.

An additional way which I think is the best to get information is to **ask questions**. Ask questions! It's a tip for life, for all that you do and don't have enough information about. Ask! That way you can get information easily and immensely grow.

I invite you to mark, write down and make the very best out of this book.

Why Don't Most of Us Notice the Opportunities in Every Corner?

I often wonder why people are in such a hurry. Everyone's running around and they don't understand why they stay stuck in place. Why change doesn't come. Why they don't break through and achieve the life they want to live.

A lot of people want more and don't do anything about it.

A lot of people want a bigger income and don't work towards it.

A lot of people want a good relationship, but don't invest in it.

A lot of people want to live a full and stable family life and do everything backwards.

A lot of people settle for less, when they can achieve more.

A lot of people wait for the right opportunities instead of creating them.

A lot of people live peacefully with doubt instead of beating it and casting it aside.

So many people walk around with negative thoughts about not succeeding, about the difficulty in their lives, without taking action to change things around. They'd rather live "in peace" with their lack of success, with the current situation.

So many people focus on "why not to", establish the fact that they "can't", that they're "not talented enough", that "it won't work" and this, instead of sticking to how they "can" and searching for ways to change and move forward towards their goal and their dream.

Most of us don't see the opportunity even when it's right in front of our eyes. We're so busy during the day in our work routine and preoccupied with "what about tomorrow?", to the point that we don't stop, not for one minute, to examine what we want to achieve in every field in our lives that we want to improve. We don't look up to see the opportunities waiting for us in every corner. The opportunities are there, but the people - are not.

Fear and doubt control everyone, so even when an opportunity comes our way, we let it slip through our fingers. How? We find any excuse under the sun for it not to be a good opportunity, not the right one, not in the right time, it won't contribute, will only take us down.

Doubt pecks at your head and doesn't leave you alone, like a little demon that tells us, whenever he can, how this opportunity won't work, how we won't succeed and that we're not talented enough. He'll find all the reasons for it to "simply not work".

Most people don't even reach the thoughts about the many benefits this opportunity can grant them, because they only focus on the negative outcomes this opportunity can cause.

Even when they do have a good feeling, they search for the negative, procrastinate and let doubt and fear penetrate and take over them. They don't take charge and responsibility for themselves and eventually – give up the opportunity and don't take action.

At this stage, perhaps after a few failures, most people stop looking up and searching and this way they never recognize the opportunities under their nose, right around the corner. You can imagine an ostrich sticking its head in the sand and staying in the darkness. This is how, in a similar way, most of society stays in the comfort zone, in blindness, in darkness with respect to all the goodness and abundance which comes its way every single day.

Most people are stuck in their past – in the sequence of their life events. They've reached a certain breaking point in their lives and from this point on they've given up their dreams, ambitions and biggest goals.

They've come to terms with what they have, with what they've achieved so far, as if it were their fate. Most of these people have lowered their expectations from the near and far future. Most people have given up the idea that they themselves can shape their own fate, that they themselves decide what they want to achieve and what not; that they themselves know what's good for them and what's not.

In the reality of our lives, a lot of people have adopted an attitude of accepting their current situation and they live in a world in which they are prisoners of their own consciousness.

Most people aren't interested in dealing with their current situation, because understanding the situation and attempting to change it might be too painful. They don't want to deal with the present and with what it's turning out to be, that's why they settle for what they have. Therefore, they give up their dreams. They don't want to deal with their disadvantages and bring up to the surface all the emotions which are related to broken dreams.

There are many reasons for this and it starts with wrong thinking. Therefore, for most of us, the comfort zone remains small and narrow, a circle we drew around ourselves and which we refuse to ever leave.

Do you want change?

Reading this book is a good start! But it's only a start. Implement what you'll learn here and you'll go far. This knowledge is more valuable to me than gold and diamonds and there's no reason for it not to be the same for you.

Read, write, mark and act!

Why I Wrote the Book

When I got into the depths of NLP and delved into the field of personal growth, I came to realize that a lot of people don't see the beauty, the goodness and the abundance around us. So I also started seeing the opportunities and recognizing the ones which were right for me. I discovered using the same principles and tools I'll present here in the book; tools which helped me open my eyes and take a better look at my surroundings. The main reason for writing this book is my strong desire to share the important insights I've discovered lately and as a result of looking at my life events from a different perspective.

The biggest discovery in my life called NLP has brought me to continue and study to the level of NLP Mater Practitioner in order improve a lot more and contribute to a lot more people.

I mostly acquire tools on the way, from learning itself as well as from everyday life, from interaction with people and from observing my surroundings. One of the things the

NLP model represents is a way of observing the human learning. I urge you to do the same. Learn something new every day, read, observe, dedicate time to develop yourself.

This book is a first of many more books which will be published after it and will help me fulfill my vision: to help hundreds, thousands and millions of people – to fulfill, change perceptions, empower, discover new perspectives on life, achieve personal goals and turn the world into a better place to live in.

Part One

The Hidden Power within You

Chapter 1

Thinking Thoughts which Achieve Results

What lies behind you

and what lies in front of you,

pales in comparison

to what lies inside of you

Ralph Waldo Emerson

Lately I've gone through some significant events in my life which completely changed my perspective. I've always heard everyone say "it's all in your head", "think positive and it will be positive" and "thought creates reality". These phrases have turned into clichés for all of us, but lately I've come to realize, how true they actually are and how positive thinking influences consciousness and our external actions.

How is thought created?

We think all the time, at any given moment we have a thought in our heads. How do we actually think? How does it start?

A thought is actually an answer to a question. During the day, and in general, we ask ourselves thousands of questions and answer them. These questions are actually the thoughts we think. Sounds surreal?

If you take a moment to think about it, you'll notice that also now, when you wanted to examine the matter, you asked yourself a question and you answered it. Every thought started with a question.

For example, when you wake up in the morning you have a certain sequence of actions – brushing your teeth, eating breakfast, showering and other actions we take after we wake up. Though what happens to us in the morning turns into a habit and we do it more or less automatically, the things we all do in the morning were first questions: "what do I need to do?", "what should I wear today?", etc. The course of our day is also composed of a thought which started in a question, "where do I need to go?", "what do I need to do today?" and more questions we ask ourselves all the time - and answer them. Our opinions and thoughts started as questions.

The immense significance of thoughts in our lives

Because of the process of questions and answers which occurs in our head at all time, thought is what constructs who we are. What we are is created and constructed by thought.

The thoughts, with which we feed ourselves, deeply influence and shape our character. Therefore, a person's character is the total sum of his thoughts. Our thoughts directly influence our external behavior, our body language and thereby we influence our surroundings.

Everything is composed of two levels: the external and the internal. We must understand that these two things directly influence each other. The internal is the character and the external is our lives' circumstances. The quality of our lives is determined by the richness of our thoughts and our thoughts shape our world.

Think about it for a moment. If you want a meaningful life, you should feed your consciousness with more meaningful thoughts – if you want passion, you need thoughts about passion, for calmness we'll feed our consciousness with calmness, and so forth.

Today I think a lot about what I put in my head and what I feed to my consciousness. Our consciousness directly influences the internal side, our character and the external side, the circumstances.

Consciousness is composed of two parts – a small part called "the conscious", which we use every day, but the much larger part is the "subconscious". It's always available, for anyone, but most of us don't know how to use it. The subconscious is where we store all the information we've collected in the course of our lives, from events which occurred to anything we've been exposed to.

The subconscious is the location of the information regarding: Who am I? What can I do? What am I good and not good at?

When I tell myself that I can and when I tell myself that I can't, in both cases – I'm right.

Each and every one of us has many thoughts about many various subjects: occupation, politics, holiday, pleasure, relationships, family, career, money and more.

There is no objective reality or "real world". **Reality and the world are subjectively determined** by how people interpret and process the circumstances of their lives. Nothing is absolute, an event that seems like a tragedy to one person, can be seen as an opportunity by another. What distinguishes people with an optimistic attitude, from people who tend to feel miserable is the way they interpret what happens around them.

The choice of what to think at any given moment is in our hands. In the hands of each and every one of us. Each thought that enters my head, is a thought I let in and therefore, I can replace it with another thought.

I read an interesting statistic not long ago, according to which on an average day about sixty thousand thoughts go through an average person's mind. The amazing statistic is that nighty five percent of these thoughts are the same thoughts as the previous day! **You decide which thoughts to think!**

Consciousness can be compared to a garden. You can maintain the garden or let it grow wild, uncontrolled. Either way, it has to grow. If we plant worthless seeds in it, it will grow a lot of weeds, but if we plant good quality seeds and nurture it, we'll have a flourishing garden.

Be aware of yourself, pay attention to the thoughts that enter the garden of your consciousness, nurture this garden. Remove all the weeds from it and see how the garden of your consciousness flourishes and rewards you in return. Pay attention to the seeds you plant. Every thought is a seed, thoughts turn into actions.

Winston Churchill phrased it in a very inspiring way: "**The price of greatness is responsibility**".

Our thoughts create both our inner and outer world. The moment your thoughts will become more positive, more pure, everything around you will change and be more positive – the people around you, the possibilities and other aspects. You'll see how the world gives you the wonderful and positive things it has to offer. You'll pay more attention to the positive around you, you'll start to attract people with the energy you're immersed in, your immediate surrounding will change and you'll receive the energy you project and instantly everything will transform into positive energy.

What are paradigms and what are habits?

The thoughts we plant in our minds turn into actions and actions turn into habits. A thought cannot stay a secret, it'll turn into a habit after a certain time.

What are habits? Habits shape our lives, we live our lives according to our habits, every day that passes goes according to the habits we've accustomed ourselves to. For example: getting up in the morning. Some people get up early, others – late. Another example – sports. Some people do sports regularly, some occasionally and others don't do sports at all.

Habits are all around us, there are good habits and there are not so good ones. Our lives will be shaped for the better or for the worse, according to the habits we choose. People think that a thought can stay a secret, but that's not true. It turns into a habit very quickly and a habit turns into a circumstance. Each habit started from a thought, from a certain paradigm we've cultivated for ourselves in light of our belief in something or from learning through our environment.

A paradigm is a thought pattern we've gotten used to and out of it the habits according to which we live are created. This is the way we "perceive" the reality around us and react to it. If we cultivate positive paradigms which will guide us towards our goals and ambitions, we'll create better habits for ourselves and from there, the circumstances of our lives will transform into our biggest ambitions.

For example, when I adopt the thought "I'm strong and ambitious and I know that I alone am responsible for the consequences of my actions and decisions" or "because of my high self-esteem, I feel great satisfaction when I accomplish my ambitions", these thoughts will directly cause me to change my behavior and my habits and that way I'll promote myself towards my goals and my dreams.

Think about good things on a daily basis, try to interpret every situation you face in a few ways. I do it using a few questions and this helps me see reality from different points of view.

Ask:

How it viewed from a higher perspective?

How is it viewed from the outside?

How is it viewed from the other person's point of view?

What's positive about this situation? How can I benefit from this situation?

The important thing is **finding the positive in each situation**, it will change your approach! It will change your world significantly! The moment we change our inner world and make it better, purer and more giving, our outer world will change!

You're probably thinking "how can it be logical that thoughts can influence us so much?" we all have a certain level of self-doubt, it's what prevents us from believing something or from taking action. Mostly, it's related to low self-esteem.

Doubt is the strongest and the most energy reducing factor, it wears us down in our inner and deepest feelings and very efficiently empties us. Nothing can empty our emotional tank faster than doubting ourselves, doubting our actions, doubting the decision we make.

Let go of your thoughts and be daring, creative, a bit cheeky; Allow yourself more! You're allowed to demand it! Demand it from yourself! Write to yourself to think big, dream big. No matter how we call it, the future of a person is determined by his thoughts. The more you advance in the book and read, the more and more it will make sense.

If a person has negative thoughts, he'll continue saying to himself "I'm no good", "it won't work", "I'm not talented enough". However, a person whose thoughts are positive will make sure to say "I'll succeed", "I'm capable of more", "I'm talented and know what to do". This directly influences this or another person's life's circumstances. What habits does each of these people acquire?

This connects me directly to questions a person asks himself. You've already learned that our brains work all the time with the help of questions and answers and that part of the processes already happen automatically.

The two people I mentioned earlier, the one thinks negative and the other – positive. **Each has a different type of question and that is a great point to start change from.** One asks "**why not to..?**" and searches for the negative or he just states a fact that he can't and the other asks "**why yes to..?**" such a question naturally causes him to activate the wheels of his brain and search for ideas and answers. Such a question enables you to think more and be more creative. When you'll start adopting this habit, you'll see that you'll find solutions for questions you didn't think you'd be able to solve. It's a wonderful way to think outside the box.

In conclusion, if we go back to the two people we mentioned, one distances us from action, while the other searches for answers and possibilities for finding a solution to a problem and a way to achieve the best.

How do we perceive the events we experience in life?

Whatever the events that haunt us are, only we have the power to choose how we'll react to each of our lives' events. Remember that suffering and frustration are always a result of a negative thought in a certain direction. We should always find our way and get accustomed to choosing the positive side in each situation, to positively view every person we come across. Our society tends to see the negative in everything: in the news, in society, at work and in gossip. It's become rare to hear people talk about what's positive around us and there's a lot, that I can promise. But search for the good and you'll see that you won't stop finding it.

Make sure to maintain positive thinking, the moment a negative thought enters, replace it with another one. You should understand that this negative thought you let in so easily, can be replaced with a joyful and uplifting thought.

Everyone experiences obstacles and challenges on the way, every single day, our path to fulfilling ourselves and our surrounding is filled with challenges and it's part of the process. What's important is how to deal with the obstacle, with the challenge, with loss, with the "failure". So as I already mentioned, the first step is **to think positive and have a winner's attitude.**

What does it mean, for me, a winner's attitude?

How do fear and courage influence our thoughts?

In order to understand what a "winner's attitude" is, I'd like to discuss fear and courage for a bit. Fear, like doubt, is a life restricting habit and it can easily reduce all the energy, creativity and imagination in us, if we're not careful.

So when fear raises its ugly head, strike it immediately! Don't let it take over, don't let it dictate your actions. The **best way to is to do what you're scared of**. And it's true regarding every aspect in life: money, relationships, family, career and anything you can think of.

Tom Hopkins, author of the book "Selling for Dummies, says **"Do what you fear the most and take control of fear"**.
We must understand the anatomy of fear. Fear is our invention. And like every invention, it's easy to bring it down easily just as it was easy for us to create it. Systematically search every fear which infiltrates the

fort of your consciousness and eliminate it. That way you'll achieve more confidence, happiness and peace of mind.

Fear is one of the things that causes us not to take action: the fear of losing, the fear of failing. Sameson Frank said **"Our greatest battles are that with our own minds"**. And here's where courage comes in. It enables you to walk your path. Courage enables you to do what you want and what you choose to do because you know you're doing the right thing.

He who controls himself is blessed with a lot of courage. Ambrose Redmoon put it best when he said: "**Courage is not the absence of fear, but rather the judgment that something else is more important** ".

Choose courage. Don't hesitate to do the things you want to do! Don't hesitate to choose! Because at any given moment you know you're doing the right thing. At any given moment you're doing the best you can, you're deciding in the most correct way, with the knowledge you have at that moment. Choose courage!

Courage is a very strong attribute required for taking action and fulfilling our goals and targets. Use it, dare, do it out of complete faith that you're doing the right thing because you chose to do it.

In our lives we lose sometimes or fail, but as a result of it elevate higher. The difference is how we deal with loss, with failure. I've yet to meet a person who fell in love and never had his heart broken; I've never met a person who learned to ride a bike and didn't fall and injure himself. Michael Jordan missed a lot of shots on the way to the top, Thomas Alva Edison, succeeded in executing his invention, the electric light bulb, after four years and more than 2000 attempts with different materials. He never gave up because his thoughts were focused on finding the solution. After every failed attempt he continued to say to himself: "I've discovered another way how not to make an electric light bulb".

No one likes to lose. A person who likes to lose is a loser – be a winner! Winners transform a loss into a source of inspiration. For winners each failure is an inspiration to win.

Failure is a good inspiration to become better and improve as much as possible. With losers, however, the sense of defeat takes over. They surrender. They stop taking action. Losers avoid failure and failure turns losers into winners.

If you cultivate thoughts of fear, doubt and indecisiveness, they'll eventually form into habits of weakness, slackness, hesitation and they will turn to circumstances of failure, poorness, dependency and enslavement.

But if you choose courage and cultivate thoughts of courage, thoughts of independence and thoughts of decisiveness, all of these will form into courageous habits, which turn into circumstances of success, abundance and freedom.

What are mantras and how do they influence us?

A good way to cultivate the right thinking, the paradigms and the habits we desire – to really teach ourselves how to think correctly and by doing so achieve our dreams – is through using mantras and empowering sentences. Mantras are powerful sentences we say to ourselves every day. Most people use these sentences in a negative way without being aware of it, but if we turn these sentences into positive ones, they'll be very powerful.

Words have a very deep impact on our emotions and on what we think. They have an influence on the way we interpret the situations we face.

Words are the embodiment of power. If we fill consciousness with words of hope, we'll become more optimistic, if we fill consciousness with words of kindness, we'll become kinder and a lot more loving. Words of courage will create acts of courage. Words have power.

A mantra or an empowering sentence are sentences we form for ourselves and say every day. When we do that, we can achieve powerful results in a shorter time.

The following are a few mantras and empowering sentences I use and recommend you to adopt and use yourself:

- ✓ "I'm strong and I know I'm responsible for the consequences of my decisions and my actions".
- ✓ "I'm much more than that, much more than I seem, I have all the strength and power in the world".
- ✓ "I reinvent myself every day".

These are the mantras and sentences I use, but you can compose your own number of mantras and empowering sentences in the styles that suite you and in the field in which you need reinforcement: career, health, relationship, money, household etc.

1. _____

   _____

2. _____

   _____

3. _____

   _____

Write them here above or in your notebook and read them every day a few times. Their influence will show soon after. Using a mantra and an empowering sentence is very powerful **and it will guide you towards actions and habits you want and need to acquire.**

The very use of a mantra and words that are preferable for you will cause you to achieve your desires and to recognize the opportunities hidden around you for the promotion of your biggest ambitions.

As you implement the process of self-adjustment, you'll find that when you change your thought towards new things and towards other people, these same things and people change towards you.

I invite you to invest time in yourself. You'll decide how much time you want to invest and which actions you want to take. Invest in considering which thoughts you want to feed to your consciousness. Look around you and cultivate questions, habits and empowering sentences which will guide you better to where you want to proceed.

The time you'll invest in yourself is the most important time, it'll reward you in the best way. Only this way will you be able to achieve real fulfillment and the faith in your self-worth in the face of your surroundings.

Jim Rohn said: **"Learn to work harder on yourself than you do on your job. If you work hard on your job you'll make a living, if you work hard on yourself you can make a fortune."**

Our biggest challenge is between our ears, it's always there, it's a philosophical struggle between the two "I" characters which always ask, nag, bicker with each other.

Only you can decide which to stick to! Which thoughts to feed your brain with and follow!

This way you can give more to your surrounding and give a lot more to yourself.

The more you internalize this, the more you'll notice a change occurring in your thought.

***

Another thing that occurs in our heads at all time is that we imagine and dream. We do it regularly and unconsciously. This is the next point I want to bring you to and show you how our imagination influences who we are and how it influences our actions and consequences.

Chapter 2

Harness the Power of Your Imagination for Your Success

Our thoughts and imaginations are the only real limits to our possibilities

Ralph Waldo Trine

What is imagination and why is it so important for success?

Imagination and dreams are vast and deep subjects, because we have the smartest, most complicated and advanced instrument there is between our ears. We can imagine anything and sail in the vastness of our imagination to where everywhere we want; children easily and regularly dream and imagine, they're better at it than adults, who are busy with the fast pace of life and slightly lose this ability.

We all have dreams, we dream and imagine all the time – during sleep, during daydreaming, at work, while driving, while on the way to a social meeting or at the meeting itself. We dream about everything: about what we want to achieve, about aspirations we have in life, about the life we would like to cultivate.

But slowly dreams become grayer and full of frustrations, because of the distance between dream and reality; because they move away from us with time. And then, most people are stuck in their past and the unfolding of their lives.

They reached a certain breaking point in their lives and from that point on they gave up their dreams and came to terms with what they have, what they achieved as if it were their fate. These people lowered their expectations with respect to the near future. A lot of people have given up the idea that they themselves can shape their destiny.

I want to share my dream with you. I see myself helping a growing number of people, assisting them with achieving their purpose and fulfilling their ambitions and their dreams as well as leading them to success. I see myself writing many more books and giving lectures in large and sold-out venues, in order to reach a large number of people and touch their hearts. This is my dream and these are my ambitions. And I know I'll achieve it! One of the tools which promotes me towards my goal and vision, which gives me strength to go on, is the ability to dream and see it in my mind's eye. That way I harness my imagination for the success I desire.

So how does it actually work?

How does the imagination operate and how can we use it for our benefit?

Our consciousness loves to operate in images. Images influence our self-image and our self-image influences the way we feel and operate.

We imagine ourselves constantly through image. When we approach a girl, we imagine what will happen next; when we enter a business deal, we'll imagine what will happen and the same with family, with our spouse and in any other situation. We imagine ourselves in our view and in the view of others all the time! We try to guess what will happen in a situation or rather **we simply imagine possible outcomes to different situations.**

That's what happens when we use imagination in the course of our lives on a daily basis, as part of our human existence. But in the examples I mentioned earlier, we imagine it as a part of a realistic situation, in which we try to guess what might happen. Imagination and dreams can spread to distant places, because in a dream you can create things that don't exist in reality but on the other hand, create the situation you invite to your life. Here is the important point. I like to quote Albert Einstein when he said: "**Imagination is more important than knowledge**". I like and very much appreciate Einstein's work and it's possible to see and understand from it how important imagination is, based on everything Einstein achieved when he imagined.

A well-known story is one of Einstein's experiments, the experiment takes place in the imagination. And in the experiment, Einstein rides a unicorn…from this small experiment and a few additional experiments, Einstein's famous theory of relativity was brought to us.

The power of the imagination is an immensely powerful force and its impact on our self-esteem, on who we are, is very big. When I'll continue and imagine myself as a rich person, a person who has influence on the people around him, a successful person, a person in a loving relationship, slowly, I'll turn into the person I imagine.

Therefore, we first need to imagine in our mind's eye our desired image in any aspect we want to get ahead at and achieve the best results in. We need to imagine it with all our senses and as specific as possible in visual, auditory and sensory terms. This is how we harness our imagination in our favor.

What is a 'horizon image' and how does it serve us?

As I've already mentioned, if I want to fulfill a dream, an ambition, a target or a goal, the first thing I need to do is see the final desired image. I'll never accomplish anything if I can't see it in my mind's eye.

I'll give an example for it – look around you for a moment, see an object or a place in the distance, your goal is to get to it. Notice how your mind is finding the solution for it. The mind starts searching for all the possibilities to get to the destination and accomplish it. That's how the mind works, the moment the destination is obvious, the mind immediately searches for the way to it, without us asking. When you decided what's most important to you, your mind will go after it. You need to do it accurately and specify the goal as much as possible and that way the mind will know exactly what it needs to search for.

I invite you to dedicate some quality time every day, even a few minutes, to creative imagination and to developing this ability in you. Imagine yourself the way you really want to be and just see it in your mind's eye, see your great ambitions, your dreams and desires materialize.

A child has a lot of dreams, but unlike an adult, the childe determines a fact. A child says "I'm going to be a fireman", "I'm going to be an astronaut", "I'm going to be a policeman". I invite you to be like this child who has faith that he's going to get what he wants, no matter what happens on the way. Cultivate such a faith for yourself.

Everyone has the desire and ambition to achieve their dreams and to reach anything they want. There is great power in the ability to see the dream in present time, when you imagine a horizon image of yourself achieving your ambitions and your dreams and when you say to yourself that you´re already there. That's when you start working towards the goal and recognizing those opportunities which will quickly promote you towards it.

Take some time for yourself and prepare a list of your ten most important dreams, as surreal and far reaching as they may be. You can write down a lot more dreams in your notebook. The list, by the way, certainly may change with time.

The list of your dreams:

1. _____
   _____

2. _____
   _____

3. _____
   _____

4. _____
   _____

5. _____
   _____

6. _____
   _____

7. _____
   _____

8. _____

_____

9. _____

_____

10. _____

_____

How anyone can turn their imagination into a powerful tool

A great and efficient technique which will promote you towards the achievements you desire to accomplish is **voluntarily disconnecting from the environment to be with yourself**. Choose a fixed time in the day for yourself in which you find a quiet corner and disconnect from the noises of the day. Turn off your phone, close the door, close your eyes and take a few deep breaths. After a few minutes you'll feel a lot more calm and peaceful.

When you're in this state, imagine images in which you see yourself as you choose to be, **as you really want to be**.

Allow yourself to see how you accomplish your dreams and your greatest ambitions in every area in your life, every area in which you want to get ahead and reach the place you want.

Jonas Salk put it best when he said "**I have had dreams and I have had nightmares, but I have conquered my nightmares because of my dreams**".

Another time in which I invite you to **use your imagination is before sleep as well as during it**. The fifteen minutes prior to sleep and the first fifteen minutes of sleeping have a deep impact on our subconscious. During this time, in which the brain works on alpha waves and you're on the verge of sleep, consciousness can be programmed and we can imagine ourselves achieving our goals and targets. During this time it's recommended to create fruitful thoughts and feed them to our consciousness. The messages are then transformed to the subconscious and when the messages are there they are available to us and direct us to fulfill our desires.

An additional and very effective tool is **making a dream board**. Find the people who accomplished the result you wish for; find the things you would like to accomplish – whether it's playing a certain musical instrument, speaking in front of a large audience, a healthier and skinnier body and so on – and hang inspiring pictures on your dream board. This board, which is composed of destination images of all the ambitions you want to accomplish in your life, will powerfully influence your consciousness. Furthermore, it will ignite your continuous action to fulfill your dreams.

Turning imagination into a reality

In the world of dreams there are no limits, you can sail in it to anywhere you wish. I really love a quote by George Bernard Shaw: **"You see things; and you say 'Why?' But I dream things that never were; and I say 'Why not?'"**.

Everything that exists in the world started as someone's dream. Think about it for a moment, until about a hundred and fifty years ago we didn't have any cars, phones, computers, electricity and thousands of other ideas that exist today. Things that developed into actual and trivial products are the result of the dreams of their creators. William Bake once said: **"What is now proved was once only imagined"**.

I wonder how much better our world could be if everyone would share the knowledge they have and together, with all the shared information each and every one of us would have, our world would be richer and goodness would be spread to the most remote places.

Every person has new and diverse knowledge, after all, we live in a subjective world and each and every one of us perceives it differently, learns different things. Therefore, anyone can and should share his knowledge with others. This way we can build a better world and by doing so, we can really achieve our dreams. John Lennon said: **"A dream you dream alone is only a dream. A dream you dream together is reality"**.

We're creators in our nature. With the help of our imagination we can create anything. I invite you to cultivate the ability of your imagination every day and to dream big. Allow this for yourself. Allow your imagination to drift anywhere or raise any idea. I say this because we can and because dreams and thinking about them promote us to finding opportunities and to finding solutions to questions which come up along the way.

Dreams promote us to action and to doing and that's how we achieve our dreams. When we enjoy the process of the journey, that's how our dreams form into a reality and form into something much better.

Every dream we have is shaped on the way to a better dream because we enjoy the process of fulfilling it. Therefore, I call you to dream big. Alfred Lord Whitehead said it in an inspiring way: "**Great dreamers' dreams are never fulfilled, they are always transcended**". The process and the path to fulfilling the dream make the dream bigger, more tangible and more powerful. And that way, eventually, you turn your imagination into a reality.

Part Two

Making a Decision

Chapter 3

The Illusive Window of Opportunity

**Four things come not back:
the spoken word, the spent arrow,
the past, the neglected opportunity.**

Omar Ibn Al-Halif

What is opportunity and why does it quickly disappear?

According to the definition in the dictionary, an opportunity is a situation which can be beneficial. Any situation that can benefit you is an opportunity. I would like to discuss this in more detail and give you a new point of view and actually, show you what an abundance of opportunities surrounds you.

And what does opportunity mean to me? Opportunity for me is meeting another person and bringing him into my life; it's an opportunity to learn something new, to expand my knowledge; opportunity lies everywhere and at any time.

You can see it in the dictionary definition itself. If we look for a moment at your current situation, it seems that also now – as you read my book – it can benefit you. At this very moment you're reading the book, you can check with yourself whether this situation is benefiting you or not. At this point, it's important that you understand that opportunities are around you and they just need to be brought into awareness.

Recently I've realized how much our lives have opportunities and so many possibilities in store; that there are always more possibilities. One of the basic assumptions of NLP is that there are always more possibilities than what you currently think. A lot of times people tend to think that they have only two possibilities when in reality it can always be expanded and more and more possibilities can be discovered.

I'm going through a crazy time in my life and I've realized that everything I think of, suddenly I find the right opportunity that will promote me to achieve it. **I learned that "luck" is an opportunity which meets readiness.** When you're ready for something new, when the situation is ripe and you think of something, you'll recognize and find the right opportunities that you want for the purpose of getting ahead.

Opportunity will come to you in every way, it's already there, around you. A common problem most of us have is that we don't notice these opportunities that constantly come to us and we even ignore them. **Some of us don't want to see these opportunities** and some of us prefer to ignore and miss opportunities which come their way. It's easier to say "no", "it's not right for me at the moment", "I don't have time", "I'm busy with more important things" and more sayings which don't promote us to a new place and keep us in the comfort zone. It's simpler not to do anything, but it's recommended and worthwhile to do something! Very quickly you'll discover that it's easy.

Types of opportunities

Every day holds a variety of opportunities and ideas for growth and progress towards the ambition, the dream or our target, towards the goal we want to achieve.

The variety of opportunities is huge, we have opportunities in any subject: business opportunities, career opportunities, at work, travelling, family and relationships, opportunities are around us and all we need to do is to recognize and use them.

Every day we get the opportunity to make contact with new people. Meeting a new person can bring a solution to questions you have; meeting a new person is an opening to an opportunity and to progress towards you success.

The following are a few types of opportunities:

Coincidence – we all know this situation where we think about something nonstop and suddenly start seeing it everywhere. For example, a woman who wants to get pregnant and sees pregnant women everywhere. Or when you need something and you feel it coming and there…it's on its way. It happens all the time. We focus on something, think about it, desire it…and it pops up everywhere.

Another example. You're traveling abroad in a remote area and weeks go by without you speaking Hebrew and meeting any Israelis. Usually you're happy about it, but this time you feel…a longing. Suddenly, on a trek or a godforsaken restaurant, you hear…a conversation in Hebrew. What a relief. You join the conversation immediately and then it turns out you have mutual friends…soon after you get ready and decide to travel together for a bit. We all treat these incidents, usually, as weird coincidences.

A story: coincidence or not?

Not long ago I had to go to the north for a certain activity, which was far from home and after it I had to get home. The way on the public transport went longer and it took me a few hours. After I arrived in the area I started looking for the exact place I was supposed to go to. It turned out the place was quite far from the place I was. It took me valuable time, but I managed to meet a good friend who was in the area on the way. After I arrived at the right place, I had lunch and my role was explained to me. I was told that the activity would start within a few hours and I passed my time reading a book.

When the designated time arrived, I was suddenly told I wasn't needed anymore, that they didn't need me and that I was free to go home. I was angry about the terrible waste of time, because it took me so long to get there and then I also had to wait. Nevertheless, I looked at the full half of the glass and realized I'd be home a lot earlier than planned.

I got to the station in order to take a bus home. The next bus was supposed to come only in an hour, so I decided to try to hitchhike. A few cars stopped, none of them could

72

get me closer to my destination. A few more cars also let me down and then I felt that the next car would be the one to take me home, to my surprise – actually unsurprisingly – the car stopped.

It was a nice couple who were coming back from a trip to the north. I asked if they were going to the direction of Jerusalem, since I lived in the area. They said they were going close, but not to Jerusalem. I asked where to and to my great surprise they were also going to Ma'ale Adumim. On the way they talked to their son and I was surprised to discover their son is called "Barak". When I told them my name, they were also surprised, but the bigger surprise was that when we arrived in Ma'ale Adumim. They asked where to they needed to drop me off and it turned out they were going to their son who lived one apartment next to mine. And so I got a ride all the way home.

This incident showed me that a coincidence is not really a coincidence, it happens when it needs to happen. This feeling that this was the car that was going to take me to my destination was clear and strong. And this is a great and wonderful example for a lot of incidents that happen to each and every one of us in our everyday lives.

Every now and then we use the sentence "what a funny coincidence", but we need to know and understand, it's not a coincidence, it's something that was meant to happened, that had to happen, something inevitable. A sequence of events that needed to be expressed.

A quote by Albert Hubbard which I loved saying is **"everything that happens, happens as it should. If you look closely, you'll find it to be true."** Everything that happens in our lives is an inevitable sequence of events and if we know that, we can navigate the incidents in our lives and shape our lives how we want, using thoughts and of course, our actions. From this point of view, that there are no coincidences in our lives and that everything is meant to happen, all we need to do is **be in constant action**.

Opportunities in business and in family life – in the course of our day we mostly meet people, both at work and in our personal lives. When we share our experiences and actions with these people, we can find with their help a lot of various solutions for the purpose of progress and growth.

Let's take business as an example. During the week I meet people, both from my field and outside of it and I assume you meet people in the course of the day – your day. I always see the opportunities each encounter holds – short term cooperation or long term cooperation and the variety is big, you just need to use your imagination.

A good way to benefit from it is to simply talk! To communicate with others, to talk about what you do, to get ideas and ask the person you're speaking with what they do. The same goes for family life. When, for example, we plant a trip and we know our neighbor or another acquaintance travel a lot, you ask and show interest in him and this way get tips for where to travel, how to save up, where to shop and perhaps even good company for a joint trip or an amazing holiday. All this is true regarding any subject. **You simply need to ask, show interest and get ideas.**

The benefit in opportunities

Every type of opportunity we come across offers two main benefits. A material benefit and a spiritual benefit. When an opportunity comes our way, we should examine how it can benefit us. It can even be written down on paper. I mention this because in most cases, people bother to examine only one aspect, the material aspect; They often judge the opportunity and make a decision based only on the material benefit this opportunity may bring, but the more we go up in the level of awareness, the more we will realize and see that spiritual benefits also exist in opportunities and then we'll understand what we might miss.

I recently joined a company. Before I joined, I examined the benefits I would derive from joining. I noticed that I was examining the positive and the negative, like most of us do, in addition, I saw that I was examining only the material matters, such as: how much will I make? What do I get out of it? What do I get exactly? I saw I was going into detail and again, only with respect to material matters.

I joined because in this case the material benefit was enough for me.

However, the more I'm in the company and the more I experience, the more I notice all the additional benefits I receive – new connections with people, who I most likely wouldn't have met in other places, learning about correct financial conduct, meeting successful people and hearing about their experiences, I myself have had wonderful experiences and I'm sure I'll have many more. This opportunity has opened a window for me to many non-material benefits.

I missed a good opportunity many times, because I only thought about the material benefit. These experiences made me realize that I shouldn't only look at this aspect and that i should examine opportunities from different points of view, so I won't miss amazing opportunities that are, sometimes, right under my nose.

How will we recognize opportunities?

We find what we expect to find
and we receive what we ask for

Elbert Hubbard

How will we actually start noticing all the opportunities around us? Well, we constantly invite to our lives the things that we ask for.

Does this sound surreal and impossible?

Actually, we encounter this on a daily basis. Has it ever occurred to you that you thought about something really hard and a moment later that same thing popped up and materialized? It can be anything and in any subject. For example, buying a car. We think about a very specific car we want to purchase and all of a sudden we see that same car exactly at the place where we are. The same goes with a certain gift we want to give someone, a computer game, an interesting piece of clothing, a certain type of girl who attracts our attention. There are too many possibilities for me to list here in the book.

Most people don't give it too much thought, but know that this phenomenon is very important. It's the power of thought. The same things like the car or the piece of clothing were there all the time, only this time we notice them. When we bring something into awareness, our mind directs us to see it. Our mind is a powerful tool, it has a mechanism called a "Reticular Activating System", this system determines what we notice and what not. The mind spends most of its time on what we don't notice, otherwise, if we pay attention to everything, we'll go crazy. But when we decide what's most important for us, our mind will go after it, until it gets it.

I'll share an amazing story with you. This book is the outcome of timing and moreover, of recognizing a great opportunity for growth. I've recently started writing a lot. My writing was disorganized and chaotic and I was searching for ways to do it correctly. I was thinking to myself that maybe one day I'd get to write a book.

The thought about writing a book is very strong in my mind. It has excited me again and again. Every day I continued saying to myself "one day I'll write a book". Furthermore, I told people around me that I was writing down my thoughts and my insights. And then…things started happened. **When you're so focused on something and you constantly think about it, you start seeing opportunities pop up regularly and this exactly brings me to the next part of this chapter.**

At that time my thought grew stronger by the minute, I felt that something was happening. A friend wrote a status on Facebook in which he asked if there were people who write and if anyone was interested in taking it further. I immediately sent him a message and showed interest. It took us about a week to get hold of one another and when we finally talked, he told me about a great opportunity to promote my writing and here I am, writing my first book.

This story demonstrates the power of thought and the possibility to invite anything we want into our lives. It can happen at any moment and it can take time. This is one of man stories which occur all the time. We think – and thought comes true. We only need to notice the signs for it and use them to see the opportunity waiting around the corner.

Recently I stopped writing for a few days to go to an influential seminar hosted by the mentor, Julie Silverthorn, an NLP Master Trainer. We studied a lot of material there and this is where the idea to open my first workshop formed in my mind. And let me tell you, the moment I made the decision, again, things started to happen.

Me and Gal, my study partner, decided we'd build a workshop together. Shortly after making this decision Gal gets back to me with an opportunity. A friend told her about a place called "The Greenhouse" in Rehovot, an institution which assists IDF disabled veterans and terror victims and that we can lecture there. All we needed to do was speak to the manager of the place. I have to say, it went so fast! Why? Because we were goal oriented; because we talked so much and deeply thought about the workshop that was coming together.

We started raising ideas and possibilities for this specific workshop and the following workshops, I saw in my mind's eye myself standing in front of an audience, giving people my added value and sharing the knowledge I acquired with them. This opportunity was created with the power of thought. This is another example, one example out of many opportunities which happen to every one of us, all we need to do – is recognize them and grab them with both hands.

What is ripening and why don't most people recognize opportunities?

These two stories, the story of the book and the workshop, bring me to share with you the tools you require in order to recognize opportunities on the path to your success. In order to recognize these opportunities you have to be ready for them. Be prepared. **You need to reach the understanding that you really want to go somewhere new, that you're ready for change and progress.**

Ripening is a hurdle everyone must overcome before they succeed in seeing the right opportunity for them. We must take a few steps in order to reach a ripening and readiness and see opportunities and fulfill them, bring what we want to achieve to awareness.

Most people don't recognize these opportunities also when they encounter them because they didn't go through this process and they're still not ready to move on to the next level. They're blind to those opportunities, just like there are people who are colorblind, and don't notice certain colors, no matter how much you try to show it to them. The just won't succeed in recognizing this is what they need.

So, what are the first steps you need to take in order to start seeing the opportunities and the many possibilities around you?

The first steps on the way to ripening

You're probably asking "where should I start?", "what am I supposed to do?", most of us want to be told what to do, we're looking for a way, a method or a strategy which will work for us. Without it most people find it difficult to even start even if the action they need to take is small and simple. An entire journey starts with one small step. And in order to be prepared and progress you need to take certain actions and reach a high level of awareness.

1. **Finding motivation and the right and deep reasons for action.**

   When we choose to do something, when we've chosen a destination and a goal we need to understand our "why?": what we're doing this for, what we want to achieve, what the intention in our actions are.

   We want to find the strongest reason for why we chose this dream, this ambition. When we construct a strong "why?"

for ourselves, nothing can move us from the path to success.

The faith in what we're doing is the strongest aspect in our actions; the faith in what we're doing will overcome the challenges we'll face on the way, it'll overcome the doubts of our surroundings, it'll overcome negative thinking, doubt and fear that'll want to penetrate our minds. Faith will create strong positive thoughts for us and will create a powerful destination image for us! Therefore, **in every dream and ambition find your strong "why?".**

Ask yourself the following questions:

Who else will benefit from my success?

What great/higher purpose does my success serve?

How will my success or ambition contribute to the environment?

You don't have to stick to these questions, look into your heart and ask what makes you dream this way, what do you want to achieve in fulfilling this dream? Ask and answer yourself. The real questions will pop up and come up to the surface. In our hearts and souls exists the controlling master. He's dormant right now, wake him up! Self-control is power. Correct thought is control. Calmness is power.

2. <u>Faith in the path and the goal</u>

A person who has faith has a lot of power in his actions John Steuard Mill said: "**One person with a belief is equal to ninety-nine who have only interests.**" After you have a "why?", believe in it with everything you have, it'll guide you towards your success. Cultivate strong beliefs in the way and in your goal and this way you'll have a strong willpower to work and take action.

3. <u>Making a decision</u>

A very important part is the stage of making a decision. Abraham Lincoln said "**Determine that the thing can and shall be done, and then we shall find the way.**" Decide something will happen, set a time, a target date and start talking to people about it. This action will create a commitment to take action in you according to the decision you made. As you saw in the last story, we decided we would have a workshop and opportunity appeared. A decision can also be you stating that you're going to achieve what you want.

Getting our of your comfort zone

We tend to stay in our comfort zone and that makes sense. We're comfortable there and we don't want to leave a known and familiar place for the unknown. It's very easy to say "not now", "maybe tomorrow"; it's very easy to simply not do anything. It's where we feel comfortable and we want to stay there. We feel safe there. If we leave this place we might encounter an alienated, unfamiliar world, the dangers of which we are unaware of.

We'd rather stay in our routine even if it doesn't make us happy and doesn't give us the satisfaction we expect to get. Most people chase after material satisfaction as an answer to a boring and unchallenging routine, but this kind of satisfaction is temporary: another luxury car, another big house, more "toys".

Most people don't progress towards their ambition, towards their biggest and deepest dream. But if we don't take the first step, we'll never know what we're missing; we'll never know what how much we can achieve ; we'll never achieve our deepest desires, the life we aspire to have the fulfillment we want.

The moment we leave the comfort zone, we'll mostly discover a new world and once we'll get used to it, we'll start recognizing the opportunities we need and this world will slowly become a more comfortable and less threatening zone. **And this is how we'll actually expand our comfort zone.**

There is no limit to the comfort zone you wish for yourself, but know one thing, **you decide where you aspire to reach**. The first step for getting out of the comfort zone is doing something that's not comfortable, start with the smallest thing and move up. When you leave the familiar and the known and take action, you start feeling differently; you start feeling the change; you start enjoying the journey and very quickly you'll feel how the investment and the persistence give their fruits.

There's a nice motivational sentence: "when was the last time you did something for the first time?" every day make sure to do something new, different, for example if you've never ridden a bicycle until this day (except for when you were a kid), start doing it. Or do the ordinary things in a slightly different way – if you have a regular cycling route, change it, dare to go to unfamiliar places. Do new things, visit new places. This way you'll start entering a new world and this way you won't shy away from change. **Make a decision now to make a change!**

Fast decision making

When we have opportunity in our hands and even before that, most people have two major questions pecking at their heads: to say "yes" or to say "no".

This opportunity is accompanied by a feeling – sometimes it's good, and sometimes – a lot less than good. Go with your gut feeling. Intuition is usually not wrong. If the feeling is not good, don't agonize over it, move towards the next opportunity that will come.

But when you come across an opportunity that is accompanied by a positive feeling – and you made a few rational checks regarding it, in order to not only rely on intuition – it's very important to quickly say "yes", and not to procrastinate. If you won't do it, doubt will awaken, take over and fool you and list all the reasons for you "not to".

One of my greatest opportunities to break through was almost missed because I was thinking too much and then doubt took over. It didn't leave me alone. Thoughts swirled around "yes" or "no" and it sucked all the energy out of me. The truth is, this opportunity enabled me to write this book. This opportunity gave me a lot more than "just a book" it enabled me to meet people who are successful in their filed and to learn from them; it gave me future friends and colleagues and it opened a whole new world for me. It had so many benefits, that I only noticed them after I took this opportunity in my hands.

When opportunity comes your way – take it. Most time it will give you a much bigger added value than just the filed it's related to. When there's opportunity, think about all the things it can give you and contribute to you and how it can promote you – even with the help of the things that accompany it – towards the goal and your dream.

4. <u>Back to the horizon image and it's enrichment.</u>

I mentioned it in detail in the previous chapter and I'd like to mention it again. The next action is to think of and create a desired future image, to vision your goals, destinations and biggest ambitions. After you do this day and night, a few minutes at a time, you'll witness things materialize.

I repeat: after setting a goal and making a decision, you should plan a route in your mind to achieving the goal without straying from it. When doubt or fear enter, they should immediately be eliminated. Always vision the final image, in all that you do, towards that ambition, that dream. The tools for creating a strong and clear image are in the previous chapter, you're welcome to go back and refine them. As was already mentioned, **when you have a clear image, the mind will start going after it. That's how our mind works.**

The universe helps each and every one of us echo the thoughts we nurture the most and at the end of the process presents them as opportunities in the material world. Therefore, when you'll distance yourself from restricting thoughts and start cultivating uplifting thoughts, you'll suddenly see how opportunities appear in every direction to support your dedication and determination.

5. <u>Creating a binding agreement with ourselves</u>

When we set a goal, a target, a dream or an ambition for ourselves, we should make it the central point of our thought process. No matter what you want to achieve, you should focus the power of your thought on persisting for that same thing you wished for yourself. You should turn it to a commitment and dedicate yourself to it, without letting your thoughts stray to distant places.

After seeing it in your mind's eye, the next step is making a kind of a binding agreement with yourself and putting it all in writing: write the decision you make, draw the desired image and specify it as much as possible, just as you imagine that same situation happening in reality. The moment you do it, it's recommended to hang what you wrote before your eyes, add illustrative images as much as possible and read it day and night. It will give you energy, a will to invest and act towards the goal you've set for yourself. That way a feeling of commitment will be created in you. And once you perform these actions, opportunities will soon enough come knocking on your door.

Exercise:

Take a break from reading for a moment, take a pen and paper and write down a binding agreement regarding the ambition or goal you want to promote (if you already have one). Make a decision now! If you don't have a specific goal, that's alright. In any case, prepare a binding agreement to implement the tools and the knowledge in the book. This action will already refine your ambitions and promote you towards your goals.

We'll learn the next steps in the following chapters and we'll expand our knowledge regarding them. We'll learn what to do once we recognize an opportunity and what obstacles can appear on the way, we'll find out how to maintain promoting actions and continuous work and we'll examine the importance of giving and how it will help us see more opportunities. Furthermore, we'll learn how to navigate towards our goal with the help of this knowledge.

Chapter 4

The Path to Fulfilling an Opportunity

**Obstacles are those frightful things
you see when you take your eyes off your goal.**

Henry Ford

What prevents us from taking action?

Most of us tend to complain, badmouth and blame others for our lack of success, for things not going the way we wanted them and expected them to. We blame everyone, except ourselves. When we stop blaming others for the situation we're in and instead build a promoting thought, it will free us from the chains we've tied ourselves with and we'll be able to act and be busy working and improving our

95

qualities, we'll do it more easily, wisely and with endless joy.

The moment we'll be in this place of taking responsibility for our deeds, our actions and our lives' circumstances; when we examine ourselves internally instead of externally, in order to locate the causes for the obstacles in our way, we'll bring ourselves to expression a lot more in the events where we are present. We can then give all of ourselves and not blame others or circumstances for not succeeding.

The doubt the environment plants in us

One of the things that undermine our actions – even in cases of a golden opportunity, and even after we've started doings something and we significantly make progress at it – is an environment that doesn't support us. Each and every one of us stumbles across people who hold us back, who will say how this opportunity is bad for us and how what we do "wont' work" and will only drag us down; that we'll lose our money this way and we'll have this or that problem.

This doubt which comes from the environment can cause us to miss great opportunities and ideas on the way and even give up a goal we've started striving for, after already making a decision and taking action.

Therefore, one of the most challenging things in moving forward towards a dream and achieving our goals is avoiding the doubt our environment projects. Most people let this doubt penetrate their minds and take over their actions. They let all the strong influences of colleagues, family and friends penetrate their heads and take over their responsibility to act and they give up. Note, that in the end, a person's responsibility for himself is at his disposal only!

Know that there will always be people who will doubt you, who will plant doubt in you. These people don't have a bad intention and they don't want you to fail. On the opposite! Most of them are the people who are closest to you the people who want what'd good for you. Sometimes they're right, but many times it's their own fear which they project on you. These people who doubt you or an opportunity that comes you way, do not understand the subject in depth, like you do and are afraid of the unknown. Like you are. On the other hand, of course there will always be the people who will support and help you. There will also be those who will listen to you and will want to hear.

No long ago I was at a family gathering, and like in every gathering a few things happen. One of these things is "updates". Everyone gets an update about what the other does and how they're progressing, where they've reached and what they've achieved.

It's great joy to know that your family members are progressing towards their goals and achieving new targets. There's a lot of support and understanding. When they started asking me about my progress and my goals, I had a strong will to share with them and receive their loving support. I said I was studying NLP and that I really liked this field and that I felt I connected with it; I told them about the many insights I had every day, and how I was developing learning into actions; I told them about the ideas I had about spreading all the knowledge I was accumulating and of course, I told them I've started writing a book in the subject. The initial reaction was a big surprise. They immediately asked "what are you writing about?" and when I told them and explained, the remarks started to be less encouraging.

The people around me, my dear family, started planting doubt in me and when I say it, I really mean it, the sentences were very sincere, but at the same time, difficult to hear. I was told things such as: "who's going to read your book? you're only twenty two", or "there's no money in it, you're just going to waste your money", "go study something seriously", "you'll never get ahead this way", "what will you do if.." and many more restricting sentences. Since I have so much faith in my path and I truly know that I'll succeed in passing on the great value I have in me, I was ready for such sentences and I coped with them in front of my family.

An amazing thing that happened – and proved to me how much people are different in the way they think and that each person sees things differently – is when one of my relatives, who wasn't present during this conversation, asked me what I was doing and I told her about the book, she told me "I'll be the first to buy it".

I know it's all done with great love; my family just wants me to succeed and find an ideal job with "financial security" so I can properly progress in life. Anyway, after the conversation with my family I noticed that the things that were said influenced me and doubts started eating at me more. Suddenly thoughts started popping up such as "who's going to buy from you?", "you won't succeed", "give up now, before it's too late", "they're right, listen to what they say".

Here's what I did to get these thoughts out of my head and focus on the vision which was the base for my studying and writing process. The first thing I did was going back to the vision and seeing the destination image. This action very much reinforced me and gave me strength to move on. Another thing I did immediately when doubt was threatening to take over, was talk with someone who believes in me and supports what I do!

This is not to say my family doesn't believe in me, but most times they'll be the first we'll hear words of doubt from, with respect to the actions we take or the opportunities we take advantage of.

You should remember, at any time, the vision, the "why?" and the reasons for your actions and remember the great benefit this thing will give you. The moment you feel doubt, go to someone who supports you the most and ask for encouragement! It will uplift you and that way you'll be able to continue with the work and the actions which will promote you.

And as you can see, an additional thing I did was I took action. In my case, the action was continuing to write the book. Taking action is a great recipe for getting out of the zone of doubt and fear and for moving forward. Taking action brings great satisfaction and a desire to go on, towards the goal.

This takes me to our next subject.

Giving it your all

Summoning all the efforts and powers in us is the very first thing we should do in every action, in every task in everything we engage in. Give a hundred and twenty percent of yourself and don't settle for less. And if something didn't work out, check and ask yourself "did I invest all of my efforts?", "did I do all that I needed to do?" If the answers to these questions are positive, know that you're in the right direction, know that in this case you gave it your all and it's perfectly fine if you didn't succeed; it'll be a success the next time, it'll be better the next time.

But if you asked yourself these questions and the answers weren't positive or you blamed someone or something for your lack of success, then you still have a way to go, you have to proceed towards coming to terms with the fact that **you are responsible for your outcomes, decision and actions.** If the answers to these questions were negative, take a look in the mirror and ask "why didn't I give it my all?", "why did I give twenty percent and not a hundred and twenty percent of myself?

You are responsible for yourself!

Pay attention, in every situation in the present time, do your best and what's most correct to this point in time, with the knowledge and insights you've gained. It's true, we're always wiser afterwards, and immediately think, in retrospect, how we could have done better if only...but even if you failed, at least know that if you gave it your all, you're on the right track.

In every action and in everything that you do see yourself giving it your all and dedicating yourself to the work; dedicating yourself to the fact that you're the master or your decisions and actions; dedicating yourself to the fact that you're giving it your all for the purpose of your success. The moment you do this, you'll notice that your actions are carried out with ease and that they are more enjoyable. You'll start experiencing the results these actions bring to you and you'll see the fruit these actions produce.

Exercise:

find yourself a quiet place, a place you connect with and start writing. Write everything that comes to your mind: what insights you have, what you need to do, what thoughts you have. Try to be responsible for the actions and the situations which didn't go the way you expected, examine them.

Write what you learned so far from reading this book and what else you would like to learn; what your desires are and what you want to accomplish, where you aspire to reach. When we write down our thoughts, things are revealed (transformed from thought into something practical), and are in front of our eyes. A quote I very much love is taken from a book by James Allen **A Man Thinketh "Act is the blossom of thought; and joy and suffering are its fruits."**

Therefore, we should write down our thoughts. This way we'll bring them into practice much quicker; we'll get the blame we have towards our environment and look into ourselves.

Integrity and gratitude

When we're in action, it's very important that we'll stay who we are and act with true integrity, out of the desire to succeed and help others while doing so. Nature and the universe don't like dishonest, greedy and evil people, although sometimes we do come across happy negative people. The universe likes to help those who are honest, good hearted and grateful.

Act out of integrity. Stay away from lies and greed as you would from fire. When you act out of integrity and show gratitude for the opportunities and other things that come your way, you see the events snowball towards fulfilling your dream.

Say thank you for the things you already have and the things that are heading your way. Saying thank you gives you power and a deep understanding that you're already in a good place and that you are progressing towards a much better place. Persist with saying the truth and with honest actions and let this way of thinking guide you.

Persistence is the key to change

What we learned so far is sufficient for the purpose of starting to recognize the opportunities around you, but if you would like to break through and truly accomplish the things you dreamt about, the things you aspired to achieve, **you must be in action and stay this way for a certain length of time, until you achieve your goal.**

We've already discussed the need to imagine, to see the desired image. It's a truly inseparable part of persistence, to see the image the whole time, to focus on it and to persist in seeing it. But it's not enough to just see the destination image, it's also important to take action in order to progress towards the dream.

After taking initiative and grabbing the opportunity that came their way with two hands, a lot of people become too comfortable and don't continue taking actions and working.

Persistence is the key to change.

When you persist with your work and with taking action, you will very quickly notice the results. Persistence helps you focus on the goal and undoubtedly, enjoy the journey and the process and learn a lot on the way to achieving your ambitions. Over time, you accumulate habits of persistence and focus and that way, use the many opportunities around you, because we've learned that opportunity is a situation that can benefit you.

When you'll persist and be focused on the dream, the target and the goal, you'll benefit from everything around you. And when you reach this state you'll be immersed in an infinite abundance consciousness.

To be immersed in an abundance consciousness

When you take all that you learned and implement it in your life, things will start moving. You're probably thinking right now: "how long will it take me to start implementing all the things that I learned"…, so I'm pleased to inform you that you're already starting to implement them now, yes yes, right now you're already implement the things you learned here.

Stop for a moment and think about it, your thoughts are focused right now on everything that you've learned; it first enters the conscious mind and slowly moves to your subconscious. You're already thinking more positive, you're already detecting the benefits in opportunities and situations around you; the benefit of reading this book.

When you strengthen your consciousness with all the tools you have at your disposal, **you'll start living in a wonderful abundance consciousness** which will give you access to all of the abundance around you, at any given moment. Focusing on action and on the spirit of things will bring you the abundance you desire. Living in abundance consciousness is a life of meaning, and moreover, a life of clear purpose which will take you towards your dream and your destiny.

Persistence in what we do helps us be immersed in abundance consciousness, but there are many more things which help us reach a place of great abundance. I'd like to remind you of an additional and important aspect which helps us stay immersed in a vast abundance consciousness, and that is – giving.

How will giving help us?

He who is kind to others is kind to himself

Seneca

I'd like to open your eyes and show you how giving can help you continue with your work, and how it gives you a lot more, in every way.

What really springs to your mind when I say "giving"? I guess you think it's related to giving something to others, to the environment. Giving something tangible. Well, giving is not only expressed in giving something material, giving is expressed in a variety of ways.

Life brings us to the point we should be in. We learned earlier in the book that there's no such thing as "a coincidence".

We came into this world to give back as much as possible. We're always acting out of an urge to give back to the world. Therefore, we should share the knowledge we have with others. Only this way can we receive more from our environment and from others.

I think today about all the things that happened to me recently and in the course of my whole life. Every time I reached out and helped another person, I witnessed how the universe rewarded me tens of times more and with indescribable abundance. Just like a boomerang.

I've already told you about the opportunity Gal and I got to give a workshop, this opportunity came our way when we came to a place called "The Greenhouse" in Rehovot, an institution which helps IDF disabled veterans and terror victims. When we went there in order to examine exactly what kind of material we should pass on to this group of people, who went through unbearable situations, we saw so many wonderful things – works of art they make: painting, sculpturing, mosaics and more along with their happiness, hope and laughter.

We talked with a few people there and got an abundance of knowledge form them and insights about life. They refined a lot of things for me. I managed to see their point of view; I managed to understand how they interpret things, what they go through and what's difficult for them. I came with the purpose of giving, before I even gave, before the lecture took place, I was rewarded a lot more and that was a great joy.

We live fast and in endless competition

Everyone is in such a hurry; sometimes they don't notice the person in front of them, too busy on their smartphones or something else. We've become people who don't communicate independently, but through a mediator: a smartphone, a tablet, a computer…most people can't go without checking their phone every few minutes. Where has communication with feelings disappeared to? Where has listening disappeared to? Feelings are our strongest tool for communication with the person in front of us. Feelings give meaning to interaction; they give us meaning for life and for our actions.

From now on, in every interaction you have with others, set aside the things that occupy your mind and focus on the person in front of you, speak with feeling and out of your heart, you'll notice the different in interpersonal communication very quickly.

What does giving mean to me?

I remember from when I was a child a sentence my mother always used to say, and it has only recently sunk in, when I closely examined my life. It brings me back to the deepest part of our consciousness called "the subconscious". The sentence penetrated so deeply into my head and now it's available to me. She always used to say **"in order to receive you much first give"**. I realized this sentence is so powerful and infinitely true.

We should give to others and to our environment out of true giving and not just so we can expect something back, not out of any interest. When we'll know how to truly give, we'll receive what we deserve from the world and abundance will flow into our lives.

So how can we actually give more and how do we accustom ourselves to giving out of a true feeling of giving? I call it "giving out of the belief in spreading the value that is in me". And what does it mean for me? I often observe my surrounding and see how much good we have in the world and how it's important to know how to understand others and when I see someone who needs help, I approach them out of a true belief that this person needs help.

I often talk with people, and when a problem comes up to the surface, I help the other person examine it, I enable them to look at it from a different point of view and to find a solution for it. We have the resources and the tools; we just need to find them. There are countless ways to give others and to share your value with them. This is one aspect of giving and its meaning.

Giving can be expressed in anything: showing interest in others, physically helping, a sympathetic ear, giving your added value, silence and more.

Listening to others

When we have a conversation with someone we give them our message, we give them a certain value. However, the real wisdom is not to only have ourselves be heard. **A great part of a proper conversation with the person in front of you is listening.**

The ability to really listen, a hundred percent, to the person you are interacting with, will grant great value to this person. It doesn't cost you a thing. It can be given at any time and the abundance you'll receive back is priceless.

The action of listening does not require a thing. You should listen without judgment, without prejudice or interpretation. Focus, really and truly, on the person in front of you and hear what he has to say out of real interest and good intention. The moment you turn this into a habit, you'll attract people and opportunities to your life. Efficient listening requires you to slow down, something which brings some calmness to you, which is passed on to the person you're interacting with.

This type of giving is so powerful, because when you implement it, you also receive the value and the knowledge of the person in front of you. How wonderful! You become a wiser person.

In conclusion, attention and a sympathetic ear are great gifts which can so easily be given and the reward you get is tremendous. An inseparable part of listening is showing interest in the person we're talking to.

Showing real interest in the person in front of us

Listening to others and showing interest in them are intertwined. Showing interest is the next stage of listening. A quote I carry with me since the moment I heard it and it's true and real for me, a sentence by Alfred Adler: **"It is the individual who is not interested in his fellow men who has the greatest difficulties in life and provides the greatest injury to others. It is from among such individuals that all human failures spring."**

Show real interest in the person in front of you, listen out of real interest to know more about the person in front of you to get to know him better. Know that the person in front of you is a whole world. Remember the person in front of you also developed and became who he is because of the thoughts he cultivated for himself.

Everyone has a rich life story, full of insights, therefore, learn from others, get to know them, show interest in them. Your interpersonal communication will miraculously improve and you'll enjoy the interaction you have with those around you more. Know that it will contribute to you a lot further down the road.

Listen to the emotions which exist in you. The act of really listening to the person in front of you will attract other people to you like a magnet.

From day to day I realize how important it is to show interest in the person in front of you and to really listen to him, out of concern and not for personal gain. When you change, the person in front of you also changes.

Another quote I take with me belongs to William Blake: **"Everything that lives, lives not alone, nor for itself"**. This saying is very powerful in my view. It illustrates the subject of giving very clearly: every living creature on the planet lives for the benefit of others and not just for itself. Everything works in a perfect synergy and we should stick to it. This is how we'll get what we deserve; this is how we'll fulfill ourselves; this is how we'll build better lives for ourselves, our children and our environment.

Tithing and volunteering

Tithing and volunteering are additional types of giving. These ways of giving enable us to give out of gratitude for what we received from the world. When I tithe out of the money I earned, I thank the world for giving me enough, by giving some of my money to those who need it. It's no wonder then that donating and tithing are important commands in Judaism and other religions. Also here, when I give, I always receive more. And the same happens with volunteering, not necessarily through an organization.

There are a few levels of giving, of grace. I can do it openly and I can do it secretly (anonymous giving), when I give from the value that is in me to all and to whoever is in need. Giving can be expressed not only in something physical, but through a good advice, lending a hand etc.

Volunteering is a wonderful way to achieve great self-satisfaction from the act of your giving, it opens your heart for a great love. Volunteering is an opportunity to give out of strong desire, without receiving anything in return.

We visited, as mentioned, in a place called "The Greenhouse" in Rehovot, an organization which helps IDF disabled veterans and terror victims. Our lecture took place. The lecture was about positive thinking and about giving and the audience was eager to hear and we gave it great value. The lecture was given on a voluntary basis and out of a strong desire to share the knowledge we accumulated.

During the lecture and after it, I discovered that I didn't just give, but I also received a lot of value from the people who sat in front of me. They taught me a lot of things, refined insights for me and raised new ideas in me and already at that stage I benefited from the lecture I came to give an a voluntary basis. At the end of the lecture we were given certificates of appreciation for our volunteer work. It was a wonderful and tremendously heartwarming bonus.

When we share our work with everyone for the sake of giving, we receive handfuls in return even without noticing. Volunteering is a great way to do it.

Free Love

Free love is unconditional love, it's endless giving. When we love, we give, but we receive so much more. A lot of people tend to see what's bad in others, the negative and the ugly. They slander and mock. It's always easier to find the negative, even though we didn't bother looking for the positive in others. It's always easier to say ugly things about others, we have so much to say, but when we want to say good things, we settle for a word or two.

Practice encouraging others, searching for the good and positive, searching for the compliment, the support. This giving does wonders and can elevate a person to new heights. This giving warms the heart, because everyone needs a compliment and a good word. I've already mentioned words have power. When you do it from a real place, worlds will come out of your heart and the environment will reward you twice as much. When you cultivate loving and unselfish thoughts, they'll very quickly form into circumstances of constant prosperity and true wealth.

Chapter 5

Reaching the Finishing Line –

A Summary and a Peek at the Next Book

Trust yourself.

Create the kind of self

that you will be happy to live with all your life.

Make the most of yourself

by fanning the tiny,

inner sparks of possibility

into flames of achievement.

Foster C. McClellan

You've learned how our thought works and why it's important to think certain thoughts and that doing so promotes you towards opportunity and success;

You've learned how to harness imagination towards success and why imagination is so important and you've learned about the process of ripening towards the opportunity.

And after you have understood how to recognize opportunities, to continue and working towards fulfilling them, your next step is how to achieve the goal and leverage the chance of success and how to locate new and varied opportunities. In the next book I'll tell you how I leveraged an opportunity which came my way into new opportunities, how I made contacts, friendships and new partnerships, with the help of which I succeeded to create for myself new ways towards success. We'll learn together how it's possible to create better communication, to connect and to understand yourself and others better.

Every opportunity is a window to more opportunities and we need to know how to recognize them. The tools for doing this are already in this book. Leveraging one opportunity into more opportunities is the way to reach the desired success.

Establish new contacts, meet new people. They are your way to the opportunities you are interested in. Everywhere we meet more and more people. Everyone has their own added value which might assist you and in any case there are benefits which can help you.

Build yourself a supportive environment which provides you with the tools for your progress and wants to see you succeed. This way you can leverage the opportunities you have to new various and limitless things.

In the next book I'll give you practical tools which can help you create new opportunities from your opportunity and leverage the existing opportunity to success and goal fulfillment. This way you can reach the place you desire. I'll include new tools in it for quickly changing restricting behavioral patterns, so you can progress quicker and harness the power within you for positive and promoting work.

Besides opportunities, the environment and you have a lot more to offer. You should know to use your mind more efficiently and to create yourself patterns which serve you, and which will help you fulfill your dreams, your ambitions and your biggest goals. This way you'll achieve self-fulfillment.

This way you can create a more correct, healthier, understandable and rewarding communication with the people you come across during the day and of course with the people you love – family and friends.

Epilogue

Growth occurs when we use our conscious mind and our subconscious. Our only limitations are the limitations we set for ourselves.

Do the things you're scared to do the most, live your life with limitless energy. Be the person you dream to be, do the things and your desires because you chose to! Don't compromise, you deserve to live in the best way you think and imagine you should.

Go and do the things you've always wanted to do and didn't do because you convinced yourself, with the help of so many excuses, that "it's not for me". Be strong and don't "eat excuses!" always ask "why yes to?" learn to say "yes", because the opportunities are around us all the time, just waiting for us to grab them. There is plenty of abundance around, open your eyes and see it!

Nurture your consciousness. It's the most powerful tool you have, ask yourself questions which will empower you, which will cause you to act. This way you'll progress towards your targets, goals and biggest dreams.

Learn to enjoy the process, and the journey, because they are an inseparable part of the dream, they are the most empowering part of the dream. The way is full of experiences which will take you to the dream faster and higher – to inspiration and fulfillment.

This book is the beginning of change and growth in many aspects of your life. Mark Twain said: "**Twenty years from now you will be more disappointed by the things you didn't do than by the ones you did do. So throw off the bowlines. Sail away from the safe harbor. Catch the trade winds in your sails. Explore. Dream. Discover.**"

We all have desires we wish to accomplish and dreams we want to make true. We have a great need to do them and an indescribable desire!

In order to learn, to do and to achieve the things we desire, we should get to know and stick to the people who did them, our mentors, our guides. In order to reach a greater understanding we need to find the person who will guide and accompany us in the path we want to walk.

At this stage I invite you to take responsibility for your life and decide now that you want more! Take the next steps on the path to fulfilling your dream and to recognizing the opportunities which will promote you towards the dream.

And therefore, if you're interested in learning more from me personally, in order to create a breakthrough and record results in a short time, you're invited to contact me and ask any question, I'll be happy to assist you with all my heart.